Here is the News!

Church Times Study Guide

Here is the News!

John Holdsworth

CANTERBURY PRESS
Norwich

© John Holdsworth 2006

First published in 2006 by the Canterbury Press Norwich
(a publishing imprint of Hymns Ancient & Modern Limited,
a registered charity)
9–17 St Albans Place, London N1 0NX

www.scm-canterburypress.co.uk

All rights reserved. No part of this publication may be reproduced,
stored in a retrieval system, or transmitted,
in any form or by any means, electronic, mechanical,
photocopying or otherwise, without the prior permission of
the publisher, Canterbury Press

British Library Cataloguing in Publication data

A catalogue record for this book is available
from the British Library

ISBN 1-85311-748-X/978-1-85311-748-0
5-pack ISBN 1-85311-765-X/978-1-85311-765-7

Typeset by Regent Typesetting, London
Printed and bound by Gallpen Colour Print, Norwich

Contents

How to Use this Study — vii
Introduction: Here is the News! — ix

1	The Global Village	1
2	Here is the News!	5
3	Evangelists or Hacks?	13
4	Who Needs News Anyway?	19
5	Further Reading	21

How to Use this Study

Although this study can be read through and worked with in one sitting, it is probably not the best use of it. As a minimum I'd suggest using Sections 1, 2, 3 and 4 as four separate sessions, before each of which you might re-read the introduction, to keep an eye on the bigger picture.

However, you could spend much longer with the study than that. In the initial stages it would be helpful to immerse yourselves in the world of news by, for example, agreeing to watch, listen to or read a particular range of news before the session. So, for example, before next week you might each agree to listen to a different form of radio news. Someone will opt for Radio 4, someone for Radio 5 live, someone for Radio 1, someone for Classic FM, and so on. You should agree to do this on the same day so that you can compare the priorities and styles of different outlets. You can do the same thing for TV news and for print journalism. At some point in the study you might agree to watch different soap operas! (read on). If you spend some time on the reflection that would result from this, the study could easily occupy you for six or seven weeks.

If you wanted to take even longer you could compare different church newspapers, such as the *Baptist Times*, *Methodist Recorder* and *The Universe* (and of course the *Church Times*), and interrogate each of them with the questions about evangelism that result from the later parts of the study.

You may well find that the reflection sessions built into the studies provide the most convenient places for breaks, and you may want to include some of them as 'work between sessions'. The important thing is to see the study as a resource for, and not a constraint on, your enthusiasm.

Introduction

Here is the News!

Good News

There can be few words more central to a Christian's vocabulary than the word 'news'. The central documents of our faith are called Gospels, an old English translation of the Greek for good news. And from that root, Christians are called to be evangelists: that is, those who proclaim good news. But how often do we relate that task and calling to the real world of our present society in which 'news' is equally important? Once we begin to think seriously about news in the secular context, a whole series of questions suggests itself.

- What is the relation between our news and theirs: between our news gathering and theirs; and between our news promulgating and theirs?
- Is being a gospel-monger completely different from being a news-monger in current society or can the two tasks learn anything from each other?
- What about the original Gospel writers? Were they doing anything that those responsible for publishing news in current society might recognize?
- Does the task of 'evangelism' have anything to learn from the way news is defined, created and delivered in the secular sphere?

And perhaps, we might have an interest in even more fundamental questions such as :

- What is news?
- What are the moral and other significant issues of the day around news gathering and publication?

- How do we judge the quality of news?
- Is there a specifically Christian definition of news?

That, in turn, may lead to questions about our effectiveness as evangelists.

- Where is the news about God now?
- How do we gather it?
- How do we present it?
- Is what we have to say about God from week to week news at all, and if so, is it good?

This study is an attempt to help us engage with these questions.

We shall begin by looking at the media context in which news operates today, and examine our own presuppositions about it. Then we ask, 'What is news?', looking at whether it is possible to define it in a Christian way, and whether there are current issues in the field of journalism generally that deserve our attention. Section 3 concentrates on news-mongering in the New Testament, helping us to make links between their news enterprise and our own. Section 4 looks at why we need news, with an opportunity to reflect on what the study has taught us. Finally there are some pointers towards further reading and study.

1

The Global Village

Reflection

How positively do you view the media? Which of the following do you find it easiest to identify with?

- They're only interested in bad news.
- They're responsible for, and perpetuate, a superficial celebrity culture.
- Most newspapers are just soft porn strung together with a few poorly researched articles.
- Television news takes itself far too seriously and its presenters are paid far too much.
- They're far too powerful. It's ludicrous that a newspaper owner can have the ability to sway a whole electorate.
- A free press is an important mark of a civilized society.
- Investigative journalism does not allow the powerful always to get away with the abuse of power.
- Reporting on disasters has helped raise the profile of some world issues and helped mobilize responses.
- The only thing that gives us a sense of community any more is our local paper.
- It's good to have such a range of expertise readily available to help us make sense of our world.

What do your responses tell you about:

- the things you need to bear in mind as you do this study?
- the questions you will want answered?

> You might like to get hold of a few papers, or note items of TV or radio news to illustrate your answers. If most of your answers are negative, on the basis of your evidence try to write a paragraph in praise of the media. If positive, try to write a critical paragraph.

If we want to reflect on the difference that mass media generally has made to our understanding of life, we might begin by reflecting that in a pre mass media age, cultures, and hence our understanding of reality, were very local. When our understanding of the world was shaped by rural culture, we believed that essentially the world came to us as a gift. Values were handed on within families. Distinctive cultures (and of course their boundaries) developed. Participation was only possible at a local level, and so our responsibilities were very obvious. Power was experienced as being centred elsewhere.

The advent of mass media changed all that. The world now is seen not so much as a gift, as something we can manufacture and control. Power is now in our hands, and we recognize fewer responsibilities towards the world we choose to receive. Cultures are no longer as distinctive. The success of English as a world language and the dominance of American culture has led to a process sometimes described as 'McDonaldization', in which the importance and distinctiveness of locality is minimal. Reality is global. Participation is possible, in principle, anywhere. Values are now learned not so much from families but from TV role models. Moral dilemmas are explored not so much in the mystery play as in the soap opera.

> ## Reflection
>
> Look again at the last paragraph. Do you agree with it? Can you point to experiences in your own family or locality to support your view? What do you think are the main challenges all this presents to people of faith?

The importance of soap operas is a particularly interesting issue. They are among the most watched TV, and listened-to radio, programmes.

Soap operas generally have quite a large cast. The interest lies mostly in the interrelationship of the characters and this is much more important than any action. Time, place and external events are usually peripheral. The authors are generally known as story-liners, and they are responsible for introducing some dilemma, crisis or issue, for developing its consequences, and for finding a resolution. The genre demands that this does not take too long, and that a resolution is always possible. The story can introduce a range of points of view, and reactions. It is commonplace now for episodes to conclude with an announcement about a help-line for those 'who have been affected by the issues with which the programme dealt'. There is, clearly, lots of scope for manipulation here on several levels. The audience base can be changed at will by altering the kinds of issue with which the programmes deal, or the kinds of resolution they find. The resolutions can be taken as acceptable solutions by those who watch, and so public opinion can be formed on some issues by this means, particularly if there is collusion between soap operas and the popular tabloid press, as is often the case. The story format gives viewers opportunity to identify with particular characters in the plot, and perhaps help us reach resolution to our own problems. At the same time, we have opportunity to distance ourselves from bad behaviour and undesirable characters as they are presented, sometimes to the point of caricature, in these programmes.

These may not usually be thought of as 'news', but there are interesting comparisons between this way of introducing current issues that call for decision in story form, and the Gospels themselves. This raises the question about how the Gospels understand news: whether as the reporting of a series of notable events or as new perspectives on important issues. The first few chapters of Mark's Gospel, for example, have been described by one distinguished commentator as a conflation, to achieve a typical day in the life of Jesus. This is just the kind of artificial context in which soap operas are set. There is usually less interest in where exactly exchanges took place between Jesus and others, than in the issue of who the other side represented, or the dilemma that lay at the heart of the exchange. What we often see is a series of tableaux setting out an issue on which the word of Jesus would provide the clue for Christian discipleship.

> ## Reflection
>
> Read Mark 2.13–27. Note the movement from scene to scene, and how each one is described as something that happened 'once'. (Throughout his Gospel, Mark uses the word 'immediately' 41 times, and the word 'again' 25 times to introduce action – far more than any other evangelist.) The 'scenery' is minimal and attention centres on Jesus' response to the situation.
>
> Imagine this as an episode in a TV soap opera like 'Neighbours' or 'Emmerdale'. What would you need to change to write the story in that context?

Those who write in a concerned way about the effect of the media on our culture often speak about the myths that modern media culture contains (see reading list in Section 5). William Fore lists four:

- Seeing is believing.
- Information overload is inevitable.
- Issues of life are simple and TV helps us to identify good and bad.
- There is a free flow of information.

> ## Reflection
>
> Do you recognize these as truths that the media wants us to believe, and do you see how they shape our understanding of reality? Which one would you want to challenge most from a Christian perspective? Which do you think is the most dangerous?

Some writers express concern about the media's role in developing consumerism, with its attendant culture of complaint, insistence on rights, treatment of people as customers rather than citizens, or human beings, and its assumptions about happiness being equated with consumption. The role of the media in developing and sustaining globalization is a concern for others. And then there are those who reflect on what all this means for the concept of truth. These general concerns find a particular focus when we come to think about news in particular.

2

Here is the News!

Although 'news' is something we instinctively recognize, it is actually quite difficult to describe or define. In the first place it is surprisingly culturally based, and what counts as news differs from society to society. In the communist days of eastern Europe, for example, news there tended to be rather austere and serious, offering earnest commentary on issues affecting political ideology. Anyone who has tried to watch the news on a US television station will realize that nothing is regarded as news in the States unless it directly affects America. Also, there tends to be more celebrity and glamour news than in the UK, with frequent reports from celebrity events and whole programmes from Hollywood put out under a news banner. British news is usually seen as part of a wider 'current affairs' agenda. In Britain, local news is taken seriously at a national level. In America that is rare. Also British media include a wide range of foreign news, which, too, is rare in America. We like to think that we've got it right and that the rest of the world sees our way of doing news as the gold standard.

Someone who has tried to define 'news' from a Christian standpoint is the Methodist writer and broadcaster Colin Morris. He believes that we can think of news as 'anything that disturbs God's good creation or reinforces it in a striking way'. The essence of this definition is that news is created as a result of something striking happening. Normality is not news. 'Nothing unusual happened in Haverfordwest today' is hardly a headline to sell papers. The only time normality is news is when it is reported from abnormal circumstances. 'No one died a violent death in St Davids this week' could be virtually taken for granted. 'No one died a violent death in Iraq this week' would be nothing short of a miracle. Among the complaints people make about the way news is presented is that if you read the papers, they paint a very distorted picture of society. This is one of the reasons why. If news is only something out of the ordinary, then a collection of news stories will inevitably paint a bizarre picture of what life is like.

> ### Reflection
>
> How true is this of the Gospels? How often do they present us with pictures of 'ordinary life'? Is it not rather the case that they present life as tense, full of conspiracy and dissension, in which lots of dysfunctional people crave healing and where violent crime is rife? See if you can think of one Gospel passage that simply describes life as most people might experience it. As you think about that, does it prompt any new insights into how you view the Gospels?

There is a theological issue here about what constitutes normality. This is an issue that underlies much of the first eleven chapters of the Bible, and can be stated thus: is it the case that God's good intentions in creation will constantly be subverted by human corrupt agency? Or is it rather the case that God's grace will inevitably overcome all human weakness and evil? The answer to this question is key to our understanding of news. Because as Christian news gatherers we shall be concerned to present evidence for one of those points of view. Either we shall find yet more examples of sin, or more examples of miracle – of goodness triumphing over all that seeks to extinguish it – and so on. As a matter of fact, most news stories tend towards the first point of view. Indeed it is a complaint of many that there are not enough good news stories to be had in the popular media. The reason for this is not usually to do with a wicked conspiracy though.

News should be interesting, arresting even. It will more usually achieve that if it is recent. You can see how journalists accept that, by the way they try to write their stories as if something has just happened. Morning papers will inevitably speak about politicians who were angry 'last night', when the article was obviously written much earlier than that. But recent striking events will usually tend towards bad news rather than good.

Good news is more usually associated with processes than with events. Someone may be terribly injured in an unprovoked attack, and that is bad news. It is immediate, there are pictures to be had, and quotes from those whose reactions are immediate. The good news, if there is any, will be about the healing process that that person experiences; the quiet, patient, loving care that over a long period will restore them. It is actually quite difficult to report that, other than in a 'the victim – one year on' kind of way, which looks more like a feature than a news article. Bad news is usually to do with events; good news with processes. Hatred is more visible than love.

> ## Reflection
>
> You can see the writer's awareness of the need for urgency in Gospel writing too. Read Mark 3 – 29 out of the 35 verses begin in Greek with the word 'and' (not always evident in English translation). What do you think is the effect of this? Is urgency something you have noticed in newspaper writing? How can events be reported in a good news way do you think? Or how can good news be reported when it is not connected with events?
>
> You might like to reflect further on this passage from Colin Morris: 'to start from the assumption of a good creation makes a preponderance of so-called bad news inevitable. The bad news, however scarifying, testifies ironically to the goodness and rationality that are inherent in the countless events that go unremarked. Once good news begins to dominate the bulletins, then what is going unnoticed is the normality of a sad, bad, world' (see Further Reading for source).

The next issue we might consider is whether news is created or reported. Anyone who has ever dealt with a photographer at a wedding will understand this question clearly. As an officiant, my view of the photographer's role is that they record what actually happens. The photographer's own understanding can be very different. Couples want their photographs to be unblemished by any kind of fault. They don't want to see what kind of mess the vestry is in, so we stage the signing of the registers elsewhere. There are standard photographs, which the photographer has been contracted to provide, come what may, no matter how inappropriate the setting. And then of course there are those pictures of bridesmaids peeping out like elves from behind a tree in a local park, the newly-weds wandering dream-like along the beach, love reflected in a wine glass, and so on. There are a number of ways in which this scenario is repeated in the news business.

- Is the setting a real one or is it artificially staged in order to provide the right background or context for the photo opportunity or the sound-bite? This was well caricatured in the TV programme 'Drop the Dead Donkey', which satirized the news media very successfully, and whose roving news reporter always took a blood-stained teddy bear with him to a war zone.
- Has the item resulted from the reporter's own creativity? For example is the story one person's response to something allegedly said by another? ('Minister, what do you think about X's comments this morning that you're a complete waste of space?')
- Is the story related to some campaign that the newspaper or TV channel is involved in? Would it have been reported otherwise?
- Is the 'story' anything more than an advertisement for some other TV programme or publication, or even product? ('You can see more on this story in our current affairs programme, "Much ado about nothing", at 7.30 this evening, unless you live in Wales.')
- Does the story result from the media outlet concerned just happening to have a reporter in a particular place with nothing to do? ('What do you mean nothing's happening! I want a piece by this evening. Don't forget who's paying your expenses!')

Reflection

How astute are you at deconstructing or unpacking the news? Can you think of examples from your own experience of the things mentioned in the list above, or any different examples to illustrate the point?

> Does this all matter? Do you feel that no one should artificially tamper with the truth, or do you think it is perfectly fair to present the news in a way that gives it context and suggests meaning? In the next section we will look at the way New Testament writers approach their task. What do you think we shall find?

Oscar Wilde said of the truth that it is rarely plain and never simple, but is this true of news as well? Is there such a thing as 'innocent' news – reporting that is devoid of secondary agenda or interest? What might such news look like? I suppose something like a simple statement of a verifiable and non-controversial fact might fit that bill: 'England lost 3–0'. But if you go much beyond that, to describe who had a good game and who did not, what the implications are for the manager as a result, what this means for England's next game in terms of team selection and strategy, whether the result was a fair reflection of play, and so on, then we have moved from incontrovertible fact to opinion, judgement and packaging. Two newspapers reporting on the same event might produce completely different accounts, in which even the so-called facts are in dispute. If, after some Trades Union protest march, the organizers estimate the crowd at half a million, and the police estimate it at 100,000, you know which newspaper will trust which account, and which will trust neither.

If we accept that reporting is generally from a point of view; that it involves a secondary agenda; that it is in someone's interest to present the account thus, then we have another task of deconstruction. In whose interests was this written? What am I being asked to take for granted or believe as a result of reading this? Whose interests are being ignored? When we're talking about a report of a football match, that might not be important, but when we move into the field of politics and social issues then it can be very important indeed. A phrase used quite a lot around the time of the second Gulf War, was 'the manipulation of consent'. A context can often be contrived in which protest is difficult. Values and opinions can masquerade as fact. This in turn brings us to wider questions we have noted above about the power of the media, and those who own it. During the Iraq War there were TV channels in America who openly declared their support for the war (as also, during the Falklands War in Britain 20 years earlier). How is the truth to emerge from that arrangement?

These kinds of consideration are important for the way we read the Bible. Some scholars urge us to adopt a so-called 'hermeneutic of suspicion', in which our reading is accompanied by the kinds of question outlined above. This is particularly important as so much of our Bible is in the form of narrative. How are we to read that narrative – as recital of incontrovertible fact, or as a series of packaged and nuanced stories designed to prompt us to believe something?

> ## Reflection
>
> If you want to see the effect of this, read an account of Jesus involved in controversy, such as John 8. How does the author write this in a way that makes Jesus seem in the right? How might you write about this conversation if you were reporting for the *Pharisees Times*?

The media is particularly good at creating heroes and villains. Editors know their readership and its prejudices, and pick the scapegoats they know will be readily seized upon by those who choose their paper. We might abhor this tendency, but first of all we should be aware of it in our media and make it part of our deconstruction process. Perhaps more importantly we should see it at work in the pages of the Bible. If you were asked to complete the phrase 'tax collectors and _inners', it is highly unlikely that you would choose as an answer 'winners'. We have come to accept that tax collectors, Pharisees, scribes and lawyers are generally a bad lot, to be equated with sinners and adulterers. And yet scholars tell us that Pharisees were actually quite similar in some respects to Christian disciples, and were often very sincere and good people. Therein lies the clue. Organizations are usually more concerned to criticize harshly those close to them, lest they be confused in the public mind. 'We're not a bit like those Pharisees' is a message to those who are thinking 'Jesus and his band are a bit like those Pharisees.'

This is an important issue at the moment, in terms of the representation of Muslims in the media. There was a time when you never heard the word 'Palestinian' without also hearing the word 'terrorist'. Now 'Muslim extremist', is almost as common. It is difficult to find a description of those who are causing terror throughout the world that does not include either of the words 'Muslim' or 'Islam', in some form, or make some other reference to religion. News media fall over themselves to try and achieve 'balance', but often this just appears as a drab political correctness, failing to correct a caricature picture. In different contexts, for 'Muslims' you could also read 'gays', lesbians, asylum seekers, gypsies, mentally ill people and archbishops. The question this raises is about fairness and balance. In a Bible context it could be argued that Christians should promote their case robustly, and that that will inevitably mean harsh criticism of alternative viewpoints. You cannot achieve balance between right and wrong: between good and evil. Others might say that it is ironic to see a robust promotion of 'turn the other cheek and love your enemy'.

One final issue in this section that we have already touched on is: what are the boundaries of news? Many people would say that news should not be promotion of products or opinions. There should be boundaries. There must be a difference between news and propaganda. And as we noted above, in thinking about the collusion between the tabloids and TV in the soap-opera area, there must be a boundary between fact and fantasy or fiction. But where does the boundary lie between news and entertainment? When Radio news began in Britain, newsreaders wore dinner suits as a reminder of the formality of the occasion. The technical advances that made TV news possible brought a debate about whether it was right to show people reading the news at all, and whether a gesture or expression, however unintentional, might give a nuance to the news. Po-faced monotone was the order of the day. Nowadays we have come a long way from that. News presenters now appear to be carefully chosen for their looks as much as their skills. Some TV stations have them perched on the edge of desks, while others make reading the news a job for two people who can interact with each other. A Victoria Wood sketch has two women in conversation. One says, 'Did you see the news last night?' The other says, 'Yes. Nice blouse.'

This issue has more sinister sides. One is that news will be chosen more for entertainment value than its potential to edify. This is not unconnected with the culture of celebrity, and the phenomenon of celebrities involving themselves in the world of social action, such as becoming UN goodwill ambassadors and the like. The other is that we may get so used to being entertained that we come to think reality is like that. (This could be seen as a spin-off of consumer culture. Not only do we have a right to be served. We have a right to be entertained as well.) A society that has lost sight of the serious and tragic, finds it difficult to make sense of adult experience. In the title of one book on the subject, we may be amusing ourselves to death.

Reflection

Looking back over this section, do you feel better equipped to interpret the news? In the next section we will look at how Bible writers wrote news. Make a list of the questions that have arisen in your mind and that you might want to take up with them.

3

Evangelists or Hacks?

We might begin by accepting that New Testament writers do indeed have an agenda. They are not simply saying: here is a completely unbiased account of some things that happened fairly recently – now make up your own mind. (Even if that is what they seem to claim.) The account of Jesus' life is highly selective. It describes, for the most part, just three years of his life, and actually most of the description is of just one week. The writers are not interested in the bare recital of facts, or in recounting lots of unimportant stuff for the sake of completeness (a series of chapters on 'Jesus: the wilderness years', for example). They are interested in significance, and their aim is to argue that in the life ministry and death of Jesus and its aftermath, something has occurred that is of universal significance to humankind. If this had been self-evident they would not have had to write at all. If all that people had to know were facts, then everyone present would have been a Christian from the start. There's more to it than that. Our interest, then, lies in how they presented their argument. Reading through the study so far, we may have formed the impression that the news is potentially quite dangerous, and nothing like as benign as we might have imagined. We now have to come to terms with the fact that the Bible writers realized this long ago, and wrote their good news using the precursors of the tools of modern journalism quite freely.

One basic element of presentation of anything, or particularly *anyone*, deemed to be significant, is packaging. Presenters find stories, backgrounds, symbols, icons, styles, settings that will help the audience to place their (wo)man. They dress him in a particular way, have him visit the right kinds of setting in which to deliver his message, arrange press conferences at the right points, and generally make sure that the audience makes the right sort of connections between their client and the wider world and history. In fact much of what has passed for New Testament theology can be seen as an attempt to uncover just that. The whole field of Christology, for example, used to be dominated by exploration of the various titles used to describe Jesus. What are these titles but appropriate packaging, encouraging an audience to see the significance of Jesus through making connections, cultural and otherwise, which will help place him in the minds of readers? What is true of Jesus is true also of that new animal, the Church. How are readers to understand both its newness and its connectedness with religious traditions of the past? The answer is to present it in a series of pictures, again sometimes with titles. There are said to be over 90 such pictures in the whole of the New Testament.

> ### Reflection
>
> You might like to make a list of some of the most familiar descriptions of the Church (for example Body of Christ, Bride of Christ, Living Stones, etc) to see how many you can find, and how different they are. Does it help to understand that difference, to think of them in terms of packaging?

The photo opportunity, the sound-bite and the press conference are also to be found. John 7 might be a good place to consider a New Testament example of this. We have become accustomed nowadays to seeing the background as a subtle part of the message. Politicians who want to make some policy statement about education will usually do so in a modern, well-equipped school surrounded by successful-looking pupils of both genders and as many ethnic backgrounds as possible. Even before the Minister has opened her mouth we have accepted a particular context for interpreting her remarks. In John's Gospel, the settings for Jesus' pre-passion ministry are very different from those of the other three Gospels. The author is concerned to present Jesus as the continuation of, and yet as the successor to, Old Testament traditions about God. What kind of background is going to be appropriate for that to strike home? What could be better than a Jewish religious festival at which a series of pithy, succinct, easily memorable sound-bites can be delivered in turn, as different symbols of the festival, such as water, are re-interpreted to refer to Jesus himself.

This could be compared with Matthew's attempts to make similar points by presenting Jesus as the true successor to Moses. Just like Moses, Jesus has a narrow escape from death as a child by being hidden in Egypt. Just like Moses, Jesus delivers commentary on law from a mountain. This is a deliberate photo opportunity. When Luke uses the same material, he goes to great lengths to say that Jesus was in a level place, because he wants to build a different set of assumptions in the mind of his readers, (compare Matthew 5.1ff and Luke 6.17ff).

Perhaps it is a little far-fetched to speak of a press conference in the modern sense, but there are whole sections of the Gospels where time and place are relatively unimportant except as an opportunity for Jesus to answer questions. In Luke's Gospel, this is apparent in the account of Jesus' final journey to Jerusalem – an account that can be read at many levels as a journey of discovery about Jesus and God. At every turn Jesus is peppered with questions – almost amounting to heckling on some occasions. These are questions that cover a range of contemporary issues with wider significance, such as the relationship between Jews and Samaritans. Luke 13 begins with a kind of heckling session that has a quite contemporary feel. You can almost hear someone shouting, 'What about the Siloam 18?' as Jesus uses this, and another question about whether some freedom fighters were in fact martyrs, to introduce a parable.

Reflection

Read Luke 13.1–20. You will see that it contains some material that other Gospel writers place in different contexts. For example 13.18–20 are placed by Matthew in a section of his Gospel where a number of parables are gathered together, possibly in the way one might organize a teaching manual (Matthew 13.31–3). Clearly, the exact time and

> place of Jesus' utterances are relatively unimportant. These sayings are used simply as raw material in the wider context of putting an argument together for a particular purpose
>
> Look particularly at Luke 13.1–5. Can you piece together the kind of events that led to this outburst? Do you feel that they have any modern counterparts?

I don't want to claim too much here, but I think it is interesting to imagine the interplay between Jesus and the 'crowds' in this way. We are quite inclined, I think, to imagine this interplay as between a teacher and his class, and yet the Gospel writers seem to want to present the occasions as more pressured than that, and the questions as more sophisticated. Perhaps the modern press conference is a nearer equivalent than we may imagine.

Another current affairs favourite mode of presentation is the video package followed by the studio discussion. We may see a precursor of this in the way Matthew deals with Mark's miracle stories. At this point we should note a few generally accepted points of Gospel scholarship:

- Mark's Gospel was one of the four sources from which the Synoptic (first three) Gospels were compiled.
- Mark's was the first Gospel to be completed, and it was seen and used by the authors of Matthew and Luke, as the basis of their Gospels also.
- Matthew and Luke generally expand upon Mark, using some material common to them both, and some peculiar to each.

Of particular interest is the treatment that Matthew gives to Mark's miracle stories. Mark is concerned to present Jesus as a figure of power, and his way of telling these stories is designed to create that impression in the mind of readers. Hence his miracle stories appear stark and almost tabloid in the impression they leave. You can well imagine them leading to 'Freddy Starr Ate My Hamster' kind of headlines. Matthew has a different agenda and probably a different audience. He is concerned to ask: this is what has been reported as happening – now what does it mean here for us?

Reflection

Read Mark 2.23 – 3.30 and then compare it with Matthew 12. Look for the places where Matthew has expanded Mark's account. What is the effect of the new setting? Is it fair or helpful to think of this in terms of 'the video package and the studio discussion'?

One of the problems we have identified surrounding news reporting is the tendency to blur the edges between fact and fantasy, by using soap opera settings and characters to describe issues. Surely we shan't find that in the Bible? Actually, arguably we do. Scholars recognize 2 Samuel 11 – 1 Kings 2 as a story within a story. It is sometimes called the succession narrative because it describes the chain of events that led to King David being succeeded by King Solomon. But it does so not in a po-faced history-lesson kind of way, but rather in a kiss-and-tell, scandal and gossip-mongering style. If it were a TV series today it might well be called 'Hittites' Wives'. Here is everything soap opera wants. Good and evil are easily identified. There is a complicated family structure in which just about everyone displays a fatal weakness and flaw. The background is one of high stakes and power politics with lots of sex interest (adultery, rape, incest) and heart-rending family betrayal. In the process, the reader's emotions are manipulated unashamedly.

The Old Testament gives us the best Bible example of another current media standard – reality TV. This is a way of describing a contrived situation in which a number of characters are brought together quite artificially so that we, the viewers, can eavesdrop (eaves-see?) on their interaction. The subjects for discussion or communal treatment can be introduced at will by the director. Usually we see both the communal discussion and interplay, and a more personal video diary from chosen participants. This is very close to what we see in the book of Job. Here five people (who seem hardly to be able to bear one another's company) are brought together in an intense situation to try to throw light on the question: how is it possible to be a religious person when we've stopped believing in a God who rewards the good and punishes the bad in this life? In this case, the director is presented as God himself. An alternative title might be (as I have suggested elsewhere) 'I'm a Righteous Man: Get Me Out of Here!'

To suggest that Bible writers use techniques recognizable in modern media and journalism is not to denigrate them in any way. In some ways it might help us to read their accounts in a new way that actually brings more life to them. What it does do is remind us that these accounts are crafted and sophisticated, and that they have an agenda. It was ever thus with evangelism.

4

Who Needs News Anyway?

It is an axiom of Christian evangelism that everyone needs our news. But is it generally true that people need news, and if so why?

- News helps us cope with insecurity. It assures us that all is well and that the world continues in place.
- It gives us a way of adding context and perspective to our own experience.
- It provides material for our human need to reflect and learn. News has been described as the first rough draft of history.

Christians can relate to some of that specifically. The most basic biblical question about creation is the one about good and evil noted earlier. We need to see whereabouts we are in that struggle, or indeed where the world in general is. Also we need to know what is happening in the world in order to inform our prayers. If the world is what interests God most (as our doctrine of incarnation seems to imply), then we need to know and understand as much about the world as possible.

But evangelism implies more than that. We need news because we need current news of God. We live in a world in which faith is often at odds with experience; in which evil seems to be winning the war with good far more often than faith demands that it ought; and where the voice of God is often silent. Potential recent sightings of God are at a premium. For some they will be the tabloid-like miracle-tinged spectaculars beloved of Mark. For others they will be more evident through reflection on processes in a longer perspective, as John or Luke might agree. Yet others might seek and find God within the controversies and conflicts of our time, as Matthew does. Because evangelists believe that the question: where is God in all this? *does* have an answer.

> ## Reflection
>
> Where would you look for news of God today? What kind of thing would you be looking for? Has taking part in this study helped you to see how you might convey it to others?

5

Further Reading

Some of the issues raised here are dealt with in greater depth by the series of essays in: Chris Arthur (ed.), *Religion and the Media: An Introductory Reader*, University of Wales Press, Cardiff, 1993, to which sections of this study are specially indebted. Of particular interest from this collection are Colin Morris's article, 'The Theology of the Nine O'Clock News', and Derek Weber's, 'Everybody Needs Good Neighbours: Soap Opera as Community of Meaning'.

This is a good place to start to add breadth and depth. If you're interested in the implications for Gospel and Bible reading in this, then my own book, John Holdsworth, *Communication and the Gospel*, DLT, London, 2002, might hit the spot and suggest further reading in particular areas.

On the issue of the representation of Muslims in the media, the accepted classic writer is Edward W Said. A good place to start is his *Covering Islam*, Vintage, London, 1997.

On the boundaries between entertainment and news, and the growth of an entertainment culture, see Neil Postman, *Amusing Ourselves to Death*, Methuen, London, 1985. Despite its age, this still contains much that is recognizable. For example, in the chapter 'Shuffle Off to Bethlehem', he has this to say about American religious TV: 'On television, religion, like everything else, is presented quite simply and without apology as an entertainment. Everything that makes religion an historic, profound and sacred human activity is stripped away; there is no ritual, no dogma, no tradition, and above all no sense of spiritual transcendence. On these shows the preacher is tops. God comes out as second banana.'

A more up-to-date, and quintessentially British, treatment is offered by

Stuart Jeffries, *Mrs Slocombe's Pussy*, Flamingo/ Harper Collins, London, 2000.

Of course, if you just want to keep reading the truth, renew your subscription to the *Church Times*!